YOU KNOW YOU'RE A CHILD OF THE
1970s
WHEN...

Charlie Ellis

summersdale

YOU KNOW YOU'RE A CHILD OF THE 1970s WHEN…

First published in 2006
Second edition published in 2010
This revised and updated edition copyright © Summersdale Publishers Ltd, 2016
Text by Mark Leigh, Mike Lepine and Vicky Edwards

Illustrations by Rita Kovács; icons © Shutterstock

Summersdale Publishers Ltd
46 West Street
Chichester
West Sussex
PO19 1RP
UK

www.summersdale.com

Printed and bound in China

ISBN: 978-1-84953-894-7

Substantial discounts on bulk quantities of Summersdale books are available to corporations, professional associations and other organisations. For details contact Nicky Douglas by telephone: +44 (0) 1243 756902, fax: +44 (0) 1243 786300 or email: nicky@summersdale.com.

To...

From..

YOU KNOW YOU'RE
A CHILD OF THE
1970s
WHEN...

You begged your dad to paint a white stripe down the side of his **Mk III Cortina,** so that you could both play at being **Starsky and Hutch.**

The biggest, most bad-ass rappers you'd ever seen were **The Sugarhill Gang**.

You never could quite work up the nerve to push a **safety pin** through your nose, but you knew you were a **punk** at heart.

You're still trying to figure out what 'Can the Can' was all about.

DO YOU REMEMBER...

Strikes

Culminating in 'the winter of discontent', strikes were commonplace and included the bread strike. Like you cared! Your mum or nana baked their own instead and it tasted a million times better than the shop-bought stuff.

Power Cuts

Playing board games or cards by candlelight was a novelty. Back then we weren't so used to the TV, and therefore didn't miss it as badly as we might today in the event that the leccy board decided to flick the main switch off.

All Change

Love her or loathe her, when Maggie Thatcher became the first female British prime minister at the end of the decade, she changed the cultural and social landscape of Britain.

Concorde

The official handover ceremony to British Airways of its first Concorde took place in 1976 at Heathrow Airport. The iconic plane, with its distinctive drop-nose, became a symbol of the decade and an aircraft we all wanted to take off in.

Phew, What a Scorcher!

The summer of 1976 led to hosepipe bans and a national water shortage, but as kids we were on the beach or in the pool and generally having a summer of fun. Mostly without any kind of sun protection.

To you, '**Slinky**' means an easily tangled, pre-compressed, helical spring, rather than an 'I'm-in-the-mood-for-love' type of nightie.

Wogan, not Graham Norton, will always be **king** of the chat show to you.

As far as you're concerned, *Raffles* and *The Duchess of Duke Street* were simply blueprints for the makers of *Sherlock* and *Downton Abbey*.

You wanted to work alongside **Dicky Mint** and his chums in the Jam Butty and Treacle mines when you grew up.

QUIZ

1. Sharply increasing in popularity in the 1970s, which building toy won Toy of the Year three times in this decade?

2. The toy version of which American cop duo's red-and-white car did little boys clamour for?

3. What was the name of the 1972 Atari game that you plugged into your telly and involved batting a white ball back and forth across the screen?

4 Revamped in 1970 and subsequently achieving record sales, what is the name of the doll – still popular today – that cried and wet itself?

5 Billed today as a 'nerve-racking game of skill', what was the name of the sticks-and-marbles game that was a popular staple of 1970s toy cupboards?

6 Which toy, consisting of two balls attached to a length of cord, was taken off the market following reports of children hurting themselves?

7 Named after a copying game, which toy comprised four different colored buttons, each playing a unique note?

8 Which popular 1970s doll had hair that 'grew'?

YOU KNOW YOU'RE A CHILD OF THE 1970s WHEN...

Margot Leadbetter was the oracle when it came to matters of taste and etiquette – 'If it's good enough for **Penelope Keith**, it's good enough for us', was the mantra of 1970s **middle-class mummies**.

You hear the name '**David**' and you immediately think of a parade of wonderful – and not so wonderful – musicians. David **Soul**... David **Bowie**... David **Cassidy**... David **Essex**...

You believed that **Marmite** really was 'the growing-up spread you never grow out of'.

At a revival of **Abigail's Party** at your local theatre, you realised that you could have saved the wardrobe department a fortune by loaning them your 'best' clothes.

Mr & Mrs Brown

Teak was the most popular wood and was everywhere on the home front, from coffee tables to wardrobes. The trend for brown and beige colours prevailed, so soft furnishings and paint were of a similar shade. The overall effect was very 'Middle-earth', making us feel like we were living in underground Hobbit holes.

Pining for It

Pine was also a wood that took off in the 1970s. Orange in colour, not dissimilar to Lucozade, the twee country cottage look was not to everyone's taste. It managed to hang around well into the 1980s nevertheless.

PADDING OUT

Sofas and armchairs chubbed up in the 1970s, boasting bigger arms and squarer seats. Upholstered in the popular elfish autumnal shades, manufacturing was of a high standard, and an authentic 1970s armchair is still very comfy today. But usually also very ugly.

YOU KNOW YOU'RE A CHILD OF THE 1970s WHEN...

You bought a Remington shaver because **Victor Kiam** told you that he liked it so much that he bought the company.

You hear the opening bars of the title track of **Jesus Christ Superstar** and you automatically sing the next line: 'Walks like a woman and he wears a bra.'

The **Silver Jubilee** mug and coin set you were given in primary school is amongst your most treasured possessions.

It's **McEnroe,** not Murray, for you (and yes, you are serious).

QUIZ

Complete the titles of these 1970s TV shows:

1 *Blake's __*

2 *Bless this __*

3 *Charlie's __*

4 *The Cedar __*

5 *Cheggers __*

6 General _

7 I, _

8 It's a _

YOU KNOW YOU'RE A CHILD OF THE 1970s WHEN...

If you knew about **Orinoco**, Bulgaria and Wellington, you weren't a geography nerd; you were **WOMBLING FREE**!

You try not to think about how close **your parents** and the Joneses next door were, given that it was the decade of **wife swapping**...

Three decades on and you still wonder about **decimalisation** (what's the point?).

You think that **Dave Allen** was far funnier than The Pub Landlord – and Dave smoked and drank **REAL booze** during his act.

Musical Heart-throbs

Glam rock arrived in the 1970s, making pin-ups of David Bowie, Marc Bolan and the boys from Slade. The Bay City Rollers – The Beatles of the day as far as young girls were concerned – caused hysteria wherever they went, while Suzi Quatro in her leathers set boys all of a dither.

Disco Fever

Disco was feel-good fun. Influenced by funk, soul and Latin music, it made new music stars of singers like Donna Summer, and bands like KC and the Sunshine Band. We never did find out who left the cake out in the rain, though.

PUNK

Shocking, unlike anything we'd ever heard before, aggressive and frankly 'just not very nice, dear', punk changed the face of popular music. The Sex Pistols and their like not only waved two fingers at the sentimental crooners of the early part of the decade, but they kicked them in the face while they were about it.

YOU KNOW YOU'RE
A CHILD OF THE
1970s
WHEN...

You remember not only the jingle, but also that the **Cadbury's Flake** TV ads always featured a girl with dreamy hair doing something that looked **faintly saucy** with a chocolate bar.

Nobody has ever been as
super cool as **The Fonz**.

Your staple **fancy dress** costume
was a swimming cap, dark glasses
and a **traffic light lolly** –
who loves ya, baby!

A 'Walk on the Wild Side'
was classic **Lou Reed**, not a
late-night stroll around an
inner-city, multi-storey car park.

QUIZ

1. In which English city did ABBA win the 1974 Eurovision Song Contest?

2. Which actress sings 'Take a Chance on Me' in the ABBA-inspired movie *Mamma Mia*?

3. What ABBA song is named after a brand of spotlight?

4. In which year was the song 'SOS' a hit?

5 Complete the title of this song: 'When I kissed…'

6 Which ABBA member wasn't born in Sweden?

7 In what year did 'I Have a Dream' hit the charts?

8 What were the names of the four members of ABBA?

YOU KNOW YOU'RE A CHILD OF THE 1970s WHEN...

'Dreadlock Holiday' wasn't a mini-break for hairdressers.

The **macramé owl** you made at school knocks anything that Kirstie Allsopp can make into a cocked hat.

You always had **Dream Topping** and tinned peaches for afters on **Sundays** at your nana's.

Next to Dick Dastardly, Nellie Oleson from *Little House on the Prairie* was the biggest baddie on telly.

Fanny and Johnnie Cradock

THE TV chefs of the day. Telling you how to knock up food for a dinner party (melon and ginger, followed by veal cutlets and then sherry trifle was a typical three-course menu) the duo commanded a devoted following. But she was terrifying!

Prawn Cocktail

The most popular starter of the decade: served in a glass dish, with prawns laid on a bed of shredded lettuce, and smothered in that Tommy K and mayo-mix sauce that went by the name of 'Marie Rose'. We all thought we were the most exotic creatures ever to squidge lemon over a pink mess.

Steak and Chips

Ideally served with mushrooms and peas, this was living and no mistake. If your date took you to the Angus Steakhouse or a Berni Inn then you knew he was a class act. (And you'd therefore be willing to do a bit more than just hold hands.)

Black Forest Gateau

The only desert really worth considering in the 1970s. Indulgent and rich to the point of triggering nausea, this chocolate, cream and black cherry confection remains popular today.

Cheers!

Watney's Party Seven made any party go, but lagers such as Skol, Carling Black Label and Carlsberg were gaining in popularity. For the ladies, wines such as Blue Nun and Mateus Rosé were favourites, and were like sipping alcoholic icing sugar.

Basket Cases

Chicken, scampi and jumbo sausage as basket meals – the beginning of pub food – came with chips and invariably a ramekin dish of cash-and-carry tomato or tartar sauce. 'He took me for a drink and a basket meal' implied cool, not that he was too tight to take you to a proper restaurant.

YOU KNOW YOU'RE A CHILD OF THE 1970s WHEN...

You knew you would **survive** – like **Gloria** said, all you had to do was change that stupid lock and make 'em leave their key...

You made your dad fill up the **Talbot Horizon** with petrol at the garage where they gave away free **Smurf** stickers.

You know that **Mary Whitehouse** was a campaigner for moral standards, not the sister of Harry Enfield's mate Paul.

You had a **pocket calculator** and a **digital watch,** which made you one truly cool dude.

QUIZ

1. Who was elected as prime minister in May 1979?

2. Who claimed responsibility for assassinating Lord Louis Mountbatten?

3. Which Anthony was stripped of his knighthood?

4. Who was signed to Nottingham Forest in British football's first £1 million deal?

5 Who became the first musician from the West to perform live in the Soviet Union?

6 Where was a nudist beach established in August 1979?

7 Which newspaper was published for the first time in nearly a year after a dispute between management and unions?

8 Who performed an 80-foot jump on a motorcycle?

YOU KNOW YOU'RE A CHILD OF THE 1970s WHEN...

'Goodnight **John-Boy**, goodnight **Mary Ellen**' was a regular bedtime call and response between you and your folks.

The **airing cupboard** was used for storing sheets, towels and your dad's **home brew**.

The **Youth Club** was where it was at.

You couldn't wait to be **old enough** to go to a proper DISCO – or even a **ROLLER DISCO!**

DO YOU REMEMBER...

Frocks that Rocked

Dresses were long and draped (Roy Halston Frowick's draped frocks, or imitations of, were especially popular) and also 'wrapped'. Diane von Furstenberg created her 'wrap' dress in 1974 with the aim of it suiting all shapes and sizes. It didn't. But it was still much copied.

Perms

Perms and afros were BIG in the 1970s. Literally. But without all the salon-standard products we have available to us today, 'doing your hair' was a protracted business. Perm lotions also stank to high heaven and took ages to set. Oh the price of 'beauty'!

FLARES

Actually, flares were compulsory for boys and girls; it didn't matter who wore the trousers in a relationship, just so long as they covered your entire shoe – the fashion for big-bottomed trews was a great step in the push for equality.

YOU KNOW YOU'RE A CHILD OF THE 1970s WHEN...

When someone hums the traditional tune **'This Old Man'**, you immediately find yourself chanting: *B-A-Y, B-A-Y, B-A-Y C-I-T-Y, WITH AN R-O DOUBLE-L E-R-S – Bay City Rollers are the best* !

You wanted to be **bionic** more than anything else in the **whole world**.

You know you're hopelessly out of date, but an **avocado bathroom suite** still seems like the height of **sophistication**.

Rhubarb and custard is a combo that you recall as the gift that kept on giving: a **penny chew**, a favourite school dinner pud AND a **TV cartoon**! Result!

QUIZ

1. What was Sting's debut film?

2. Who was the disembodied voice narrating Agatha Christie's *And Then There Were None*?

3. Who directed *Death Wish*?

4. What was the sequel to *Love Story*?

5. Who sang the title song on the Disney movie *The Aristocats*?

6 Who did Olivia Newton-John play in *Grease*?

7 Who played opposite Audrey Hepburn in *Robin and Marian*?

8 What was Peter Ustinov's first film as Hercule Poirot?

Answers: 1. *Quadrophenia* **2.** Orson Welles **3.** Michael Winner **4.** *Oliver's Story* **5.** Maurice Chevalier **6.** Sandy **7.** Sean Connery **8.** *Death on the Nile*

43

YOU KNOW YOU'RE A CHILD OF THE 1970s WHEN...

You used to have a cassette of **Derek and Clive** that you kept hidden from your mum.

You tell anyone who'll listen that **Carl Douglas** could kick Jackie Chan's or Jet Li's butt.

You find yourself scouring eBay for that elusive **1970s World Cup Squad** coin collection or *The Sun's* football **stamp album**.

You think radio peaked with **Kenny Everett** and the genius that was **Captain Kremmen**.

Platforms

Again, a unisex wardrobe staple, but for chaps, wearing a shoe that was a high heel of sorts was new territory. Kind of essential, though, as you needed the height to stop you breaking your neck by tripping up on your flares or bell-bottoms.

Fabricating

Velour and Terrycloth became popular fabrics used in the making of men's shirts later in the decade. This put you in mind of the flock wallpaper in your local curry house every time you got dressed.

CHEST HAIR AND MEDALLIONS

It was all about how much of a rug your chest could sprout and then how well you decorated it with bling. Now a cliché of the decade, you can easily spot a child of the 1970s on a beach today.

If you heard your parents say that they needed to call in a professional for a household task, you assumed that **Bodie** or **Doyle** were going to rock up to fix the boiler or **crazy pave** the garden.

You can't believe you were ever engrossed in a soap opera about a **North Sea ferry** starring Kate O'Mara.

You still maintain that there was nothing wrong with queuing for eleven hours to see **Star Wars**.

All the **great songs** of your childhood are readily available on **free CDs** with the weekend newspapers.

ONLY A CHILD OF THE 1970s WILL KNOW...

1. A delicious combination of fudge, chocolate and rum flavour, what was the Cadbury's bar named after a dance?

2. What was the name of the sizzling candy that came in a packet with a picture of the Moon on it?

3. Actor Gary Myers advertised which brand of boxed chocolates in the 1970s?

4 Which chocolate bar, named after a wild animal, was launched in 1976?

5 Which crisp manufacturer produced salt and vinegar Chipsticks?

6 Made of chewy caramel covered in milk chocolate, which choc bar first appeared in 1970?

7 In which year was Cadbury's Creme Egg launched?

8 Which chocolate bar, named after the abbreviation for a small breed of dog, was launched in 1976?

Answers: 1. Rumba **2.** Space Dust **3.** Milk Tray (he was the Milk Tray Man of the 1970s) **4.** Lion Bar **5.** Smiths **6.** Curly Wurly **7.** 1971 **8.** Yorkie

51

YOU KNOW YOU'RE
A CHILD OF THE
1970s
WHEN...

Only the most **middle class**
of your schoolmates' parents
ever served up butterscotch
Angel Delight.

Somewhere, in a safely guarded keepsake box, is your '**Rock Against Racism**' badge.

You know that **Tavares** is NOT a tropical disease.

You spent the summer living in your **tank top**.

DO YOU REMEMBER...

Magpie

ITV's cooler version of *Blue Peter* — Tommy Boyd, Mick Robertson and Jenny Hanley were some of the presenters on the magazine show for teens. Who still sings the theme tune when they spot a black and white birdy?

Grange Hill

Launching in 1978 and lasting 30 years, the likes of Trisha Yates, Tucker and Doyle made us all want to go to this cool school. Parents were less impressed, with some banning it on account of it leading their offspring astray via daring storylines entailing bunking off and, later, drug addiction.

Lizzie Dripping

Set in the village of Little Hemlock, a young girl with a fanciful imagination would meet with a bad-tempered witch that only she could see and hear. Strangely compelling, we were intrigued by the idea that perhaps a grumpy witch might rock up in the local park or churchyard.

Rentaghost

In 1976, this comedy about ghosts who could be rented out to haunt places was a big hit. Remember naughty Mr Claypole, Dobbin the Pantomime Horse and Miss Popov? Spooktacular fun!

Rainbow

Zippy, Bungle and George took us up above the streets and houses, and lifted our little hearts up just as high with their daft antics, songs and stories. It's hard to pinpoint exactly what the show's charm was, but there was something hypnotically 'Night Garden-ish' about it.

Multi-Coloured Swap Shop

The BBC's alternative to *Tiswas*, this Saturday morning show, hosted by Noel Edmonds, enabled you to swap your stuff, see celebs being interviewed and have a giggle at Posh Paws the dinosaur and whatever Cheggers (Keith Chegwin) was up to. Usually something that involved getting wet or covered in gunk.

YOU KNOW YOU'RE
A CHILD OF THE
1970s
WHEN...

If asked to name a celebrity
couple, you instantly reply:
'Farrah Fawcett-Majors and
Lee Majors.'

You begged your mum to
knit you a **Clanger**.

You close your eyes and can still
taste **Mint Cracknel**, Amazin'
Raisin and **Aztec bars**.

Your adolescent fantasies involved
Anthea Redfern, Marie Osmond
and the blonde one from **ABBA**
(and sometimes all three).

QUIZ

1. Who wrote *The Hitchhiker's Guide to the Galaxy*?

2. Who wrote *Watership Down*?

3. What birds did Colleen McCullough write about?

4. Who wrote the horror novel, *Carrie*?

5. *The Lorax* was written by which famous children's author?

58

6 What number Charing Cross Road did Helene Hanff write about?

7 What 'day' did Frederick Forsyth write about?

8 Which biblical pair was the title of a Jeffrey Archer novel?

YOU KNOW YOU'RE A CHILD OF THE 1970s WHEN...

You thought that the three funniest men in the whole wide world were **Tim Brooke-Taylor**, **Graeme Garden** and **Bill Oddie**.

You were scared stiff of the
Bermuda Triangle.

The latest advances in consumer
technology always came from
K-Tel or **Ronco**.

You used to bounce about on
a **space hopper**. Now you're
starting to resemble one.

DO YOU REMEMBER...

The Onedin Line

Classic BBC drama series set in nineteenth-century Liverpool, following the changing fortunes of the go-getting Captain James Onedin and his family was a big favourite. With its belter of a theme tune, nicked from a ballet, the nautical doings of the Onedins kept us entertained throughout the decade.

That's Life!

In this first consumer programme, Esther Rantzen was your hostess. Although light-hearted (there was something of a fixation with talking dogs and plus-size vegetables), the show also campaigned – very effectively – for things like child organ donors and the wearing of seat belts.

THE BENNY HILL SHOW

You simply couldn't get away with it now but back in the day young girls running around in nurses' uniforms while sleazy old men chased them passed for entertainment. 'Hill's Angels' had a huge fan club and the humour, while not exactly subtle, was definitely of the LOL variety.

YOU KNOW YOU'RE A CHILD OF THE 1970s WHEN...

Your **first taste** of alcohol came from a lukewarm can of **Top Deck** shandy.

Summer holidays were spent riding your **Raleigh Chopper** and imagining yourself as Barry Sheene or **Evel Knievel**.

You once thought that **The Fonz** and **Alvin Stardust** were the hardest men on the planet.

You wouldn't go out without first checking your **mood ring** and your **biorhythms**.

1. Which biscuit was advertised with the tagline, 'a drink's too wet without one'?

2. What was 'just enough to give your kids a treat'?

3. 'Anything else just isn't tennis' – what was the product?

4. What was 'bigger than the average soup'?

5 Which brand promised that you would 'cross over to a better figure'?

6 Which aftershave was for 'men who don't have to try too hard'?

7 Which brand claimed that 'every bubble's passed its fizzical'?

8 Which hairspray asked: 'Is she or isn't she?'

YOU KNOW YOU'RE A CHILD OF THE 1970s WHEN...

You spent your childhood kitted out in clothes from **C&A** – if you were that lucky.

You baffle your kids by doing
Frank Spencer impersonations –
and then confuse them further
by claiming you're 'better than
Mike Yarwood' at it.

Your idea of a supermodel
was an **Airfix** 1:72 scale
B-17 Flying Fortress.

You remember being told that
avocado was the new black.

DO YOU REMEMBER...

Monty Python and the Holy Grail

Causing a very crotchety reaction in some quarters on account of its religious irreverence, in 1975 the Python team saw bits of their script being turned into catchphrases all over the country. They were very naughty boys!

Jaws

We all looked carefully before we swam in the sea after 1975, just in case there was a ruddy great big white loitering around the shallows, waiting to tear us limb from limb. Spielberg's big fish certainly did big box office.

STAR WARS

Back in 1977, Luke Skywalker was God and you wanted to have your own C-3PO robot. (And you hated getting up for a wee in the night because your mum's quilted black housecoat, hanging on the back of the bathroom door, made you think of Darth Vader.)

YOU KNOW YOU'RE A CHILD OF THE 1970s WHEN...

You used to kid yourself that you looked like **Bodie**, and your best mate looked like **Doyle**.

You grew up wanting to be **Jason King**, the Six Million Dollar Man or **Charlie George** – if you were a boy...

... and **Wonder Woman** or **Kate Bush** if you were a girl.

You wore nail varnish, sequins and **glitter** – and didn't feel any **less of a man** for doing so.

QUIZ

ONLY A CHILD OF THE 1970s WILL KNOW...

1 Which group had a hit with 'Mary's Boy Child'?

2 Who sang the hit 'Save Your Kisses for Me'?

3 'Don't Give Up on Us' was a hit for which David?

4 Who wanted to 'teach the world to sing'?

5 Who was 'Sailing' in the charts?

6 John Travolta and Olivia Newton-John sang about what kind of nights?

7 The Pipes and Drums and Military Band of the Royal Scots Dragoon Guards had a hit with which song?

8 Who were 'Under the Moon of Love'?

YOU KNOW YOU'RE A CHILD OF THE 1970s WHEN...

Sophistication was **pineapple** and cheese on sticks, and a glass of warm **Cinzano**.

You've never forgiven your
parents for exposing you to their
Roger Whittaker collection.

Men's grooming products
consisted of **soap on a rope**,
a can of Cossack hairspray
and a bottle of **Hai Karate**
or Blue Stratos.

You find yourself muttering the
catchphrases 'I 'ate you, Butler',
'Nice one, Cyril' and
'Uh-Oh Chongo'.

DO YOU REMEMBER...

Kevin Keegan

The player of the decade, Kev's prowess on the pitch was almost as impressive as his shaggy perm. Winning three First Division titles while at Liverpool FC, there wasn't a boy alive under ten who didn't want to be KK.

George Best

Boys over the age of ten wanted to be Bestie. One of the greatest players of all time, by the 1970s he was hitting the headlines for the wrong reasons: 'In 1969 I gave up women and alcohol – it was the worst 20 minutes of my life.'

RED RUM

The dream horse who made the evil Grand National course look effortless, Red Rum won the race on three occasions, earning him a place in the record books, mass public affection and more polos than he could shake a hoof at.

YOU KNOW YOU'RE A CHILD OF THE 1970s WHEN...

Your idea of an 'illegal download' was taping songs off the radio with a **hand-held microphone.**

You resented the fact
that everyone was **on strike**
except schoolteachers.

You can still play 'Stairway to
Heaven' on your tennis racket.

You remember reading the **chess
results** in the sports pages of
national newspapers.

QUIZ

ONLY A CHILD OF THE 1970s WILL KNOW...

1 What was the name of the department store in *Are You Being Served??*

2 Robert Lindsay starred as Wolfie in which sitcom?

3 Who played Frank in *Some Mothers Do 'Ave 'Em?*

4 Who did Bill Pertwee play in *Dad's Army?*

5 Melvyn Hayes starred as 'Gloria' in which sitcom?

6 What was the name of Manuel's rat in *Fawlty Towers*?

7 What kind of 'birds' shared a flat in a 1970s sitcom?

8 Set in a hospital, complete the sitcom title: *Only When __?*

Answers: 1. Grace Brothers **2.** *Citizen Smith* **3.** Michael Crawford **4.** Warden Hodges **5.** *It Ain't Half Hot Mum* **6.** Basil **7.** Liver Birds **8.** *I Laugh*

83

YOU KNOW YOU'RE A CHILD OF THE 1970s WHEN...

A 'home cinema system' consisted of a **Super-8** projector and a white sheet.

The biggest decision you ever had to make was: 'Donny Osmond or David Cassidy?'

You were a member of the official *Planet of the Apes* fan club and the **KISS Army**.

You still occasionally crave a bottle of **Cresta** ('It's frothy, man!').

Space Invaders

By today's standards, this late 1970s arcade game seems hopelessly clunky and unsophisticated, but back then it was just the most exciting thing EVER! Shooting from a little green ship and zapping the odd-looking little space crabs provided as much fun as you could make 10 p last for.

Gadget in Goal

Launched in 1977, Mattel's iconic electronic hand-held Football game was the business. Pretty unsophisticated by today's standards, it consisted of simple electronic dots and lines, but in the 1970s it was thrilling stuff.

Wired for Sound

The Sony Walkman Personal Music Player arrived at the end of the decade and, oh boy, how we all lusted after it! And unlike the Personal CD Player that came later, tapes didn't skip when you went out jogging. Interestingly, the prototype was created so that Sony co-founder, Masaru Ibuka, could listen to opera while travelling.

VHS vs Betamax

The late 1970s also saw the launch of the first video recorder and, with it, the ruck between VHS and Betamax models. Although the Betamax format was superior to VHS, the limited one-hour recording tapes (versus four hours for VHS) helped to consign the format to the scrapheap.

SodaStream

'Get busy with the fizzy' – the SodaStream was a brilliant novelty as a 1970s kid. Messing with mini gas canisters and making your own lemonade was just the coolest thing to do when you were a nipper.

YOU KNOW YOU'RE
A CHILD OF THE
1970s
WHEN...

You spent a month with
your wrist in plaster after a
horrific **Clackers** accident.

You think **Dick Emery** made
a more convincing woman
than David Walliams.

You put your **atrocious
spelling** down to all those
Slade song titles.

Having **G Plan** furniture,
wall-to-wall carpeting,
a **yucca** plant and a through
lounge confirmed that your
family were **middle class**.

QUIZ

1. Which member of the Royal Family got married on 14 November 1973?

2. The President of Cameroon gave the Queen an unusual gift in in 1972 to mark her silver wedding anniversary. What was the 'enormous' gift?

3. The only time the Queen has had to interrupt an overseas tour was in 1974, during a tour of Australia and Indonesia. Why?

4 To the nearest thousand, how many miles did the Queen travel during the 1977 Silver Jubilee year?

5 What was Derby granted in honour of Her Majesty's Silver Jubilee?

6 Which royal baby was born on 15 November 1977?

7 Which royal celebrated their eighteenth birthday on 19 February 1978?

8 Who was Princess Anne's first husband?

YOU KNOW YOU'RE A CHILD OF THE 1970s WHEN...

Your dream car was a
Ford Capri 2000 XL – that or
a Lunar Roving Vehicle.

You looked forward to watching **Ask the Family** and identifying the close-up, black-and-white photo of a comb or **a pencil sharpener**.

You used to wear **tartan** – and you'd never even been to Scotland.

You once started each day with a bowl of **Puffa Puffa Rice** or **Golden Nuggets**.

Ford Mk III Cortina

The best-selling car of the early part of the decade. The 1976 Mk IV Cortina took over that position until the end of the 1970s, thanks mostly to square-rigged styling and an even larger range.

Austin 1100 and 1300

Thanks to the A-Series engines, the Austin 1100 and 1300 rivalled the Mini for fun factor. Very popular, it was one of the country's most desired cars by the early 1970s, but production ended in 1974.

MORRIS MARINA

One of the most popular cars of the decade, this was British Leyland's fight back against the Cortina. The rear-wheel drive, which many thought a backward step, actually proved to be a selling point.

YOU KNOW YOU'RE A CHILD OF THE 1970s WHEN...

You'd spend hours in
Miss Selfridge discussing
the various merits of baggies,
parallels, **bell-bottoms** or flares.

You remember 'Cod Wars'
and your parents reassuring you
that Iceland would never resort to
'the nuclear option'.

All your pocket money was spent
on **Pink Panther** bars, Bazooka
Joes and *Countdown* comics.

You not only know what
carbon paper is, but you used it
regularly in your first office job.

QUIZ

ONLY A CHILD OF THE 1970s WILL KNOW...

1. Which jazz man died in New York, in 1974, at the age of 75?

2. Which punk legend was found dead from a suspected heroin overdose in February 1979?

3. What was the stage name of the famous former stripper who died in 1970?

4. Which British-born silent funny man died on Christmas day 1977 in Switzerland?

5 Which prolific author and playwright died in January 1976?

6 Which music legend and actor died on 16 August 1977?

7 In the year 1973 the world lost a great artist. Who?

8 Succeeded by his third wife, which Argentine leader died in 1974?

YOU KNOW YOU'RE A CHILD OF THE 1970s WHEN...

You could once enthrall
30 classmates just by
showing off your new **Blakey's**.

Marc Bolan and his feather boa got you all confused about your **sexuality**... at just the wrong time of life.

There was a universally and socially understood jeans hierarchy: **Levi's**, Wranglers, Lee, Brutus Gold... then **Keynote**.

You can't quite convey to your children just how good a **Lord Toffingham** ice lolly tasted.

DO YOU REMEMBER...

School Milk

It came in little bottles with a straw poked through the top of the foil stopper. It was usually delivered first thing in the morning, and then left next to the radiator in the classroom until we had to drink it just before we left. By which time it was yoghurt.

1970s Punishments

The cane was still being used, which seemed to give teachers the green light to act in a generally violent and psychopathic manner: throwing chalk, books and blackboard rubbers at any pupil they felt wasn't giving them their full attention. Apparently, it hurt them more than it hurt us. Liars.

SCHOOL DINNERS

Well, they were hot. Mostly. Although mashed potato, served in ice cream-scooped balls, was always cold in the middle. Liver in a nasty gravy was a regular feature, with tinned butter beans passing as vegetables. Lumpy custard with skin on and various milk puddings were staples of the dessert menu.

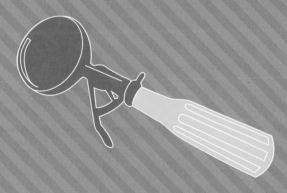

YOU KNOW YOU'RE A CHILD OF THE 1970s WHEN...

You managed to sneak in, underage, to see *The Exorcist* – and then spent many sleepless nights wishing you hadn't.

You and your friends had
a gang based around
The Tomorrow People.

The **children's TV** presenters
were as old as your dad,
not your big brother.

You'll never forget the day
the **Phantom Flan Flinger**
attacked the St Winifred's
School Choir on *Tiswas*.

QUIZ

ONLY A CHILD OF THE 1970s WILL KNOW...

1. Which puppet's catch phrase was 'Ha ha ha! Boom boom!'?

2. What was Sooty and Sweep's panda friend called?

3. Which famous puppet TV show began in 1976?

4. Hartley Hare was a puppet in which TV show?

5 Ray Alan was a ventriloquist whose snooty puppet was called Lord-?

6 Who was Nookie Bear's puppeteer?

7 Who did Rod Hull's puppet Emu famously attack during an interview?

8 What kind of creature was the puppet George from kids' TV show, *Rainbow*?

Answers: 1. Basil Brush **2.** Soo **3.** *The Muppet Show*
4. Pipkins **5.** Charles **6.** Roger De Courcey
7. Michael Parkinson **8.** Hippopotamus

107

YOU KNOW YOU'RE A CHILD OF THE 1970s WHEN...

You don't consider **dark brown** and **cheesecloth** to be crimes against fashion.

TV ad breaks regularly featured useful public information films warning you about the **perils** of playing near **railway lines** and accepting lifts from strangers.

You think Queen's **'Bohemian Rhapsody'** is the greatest pop video ever made.

You attribute your short-term memory loss to all the chemicals in the **Parma Violets** that you scoffed down back then.

DO YOU REMEMBER...

Funny Girl

Comedy was male-dominated but bucking the trend was Victoria Wood who, having won TV talent show *New Faces* in 1974, went on to make us laugh until our sides split with her brilliantly observed humour, superbly timed delivery and hilarious songs.

Comedy Carrott

When Jasper Carrott released the novelty song 'Funky Moped' in 1975, he had no idea that the B-side, a mickey-take of kids' TV show *The Magic Roundabout*, would prove to be the bigger hit. And we all knew it word for rude word. Boing!

Laughing Les Dawson

Deadpan delivery and more mother-in-law jokes than you could shake a stick at; Les's gift for gurning helped him to become one of the most prolific comedians of the decade. I'm not saying my mother-in-law's fat, but when she wears a red dress, people try to post a letter in her...

'Awful' Dick Emery

With his catchphrase of 'Ooh you are awful... but I like you!', the *Dick Emery Show* ran throughout the 1970s. Using sketches rather than stand-up, Emery was a gifted actor and comic who made for (mostly) good family fun.

The Two Ronnies

A sketch show that made the pair household names: Ronnie Corbett and Ronnie Barker were a comedic match made in heaven. Who can forget 'Four Candles' and the *Mastermind* contestant whose specialist subject was answering the question before last?

Morecambe and Wise

Coming a bit before the Two Ronnies, this funny pair's USP was getting their special guests to appear in their sketches. Newsreaders performing 'There is Nothing Like a Dame' remains TV comedy gold.

YOU KNOW YOU'RE
A CHILD OF THE
1970s
WHEN...

You and your mates all had a favourite 'angel' from *Charlie's Angels* and you'd spend hours arguing who was the tastiest.

Your child's weekly **pocket money** is more than your first weekly pay packet.

You wished you could be adopted by the **Partridge family**.

Staying in a **half-built hotel** in Magaluf or Benidorm was considered **exotic**.

QUIZ

ONLY A CHILD OF THE 1970s WILL KNOW...

1 Who was Nixon's White House Chief of Staff at the height of the Watergate Scandal?

2 Which female MP did Jack Straw replace as MP for Blackburn?

3 Who made a precocious speech, aged 16, at the 1977 Tory Party Conference?

4 The Equal Opportunities Commission was set up to implement which act?

5 Which dictator was deposed in Cambodia in 1979?

6 In which government department was Margaret Thatcher a minister before she became leader of the Conservative Party?

7 Who stood down as Labour Party leader in 1976?

8 Which 1970s prime minister was nicknamed 'Grocer'?

YOU KNOW YOU'RE A CHILD OF THE 1970s WHEN...

If you were lucky enough to have a computer it was the **Atari VCS** with 128 colours.

You really believed that
Gary Numan was radical,
avant-garde and rebellious.

You once thought that the sight
of **Terry Scott** dressed as a
schoolboy was funny (and not
deeply disturbing).

You can sing the words
and perform all the actions to
'**The Lumberjack Song**'.

DO YOU REMEMBER...

Look-in

One for boys and girls, this magazine highlighted kids' shows in ITV's programme listings. *Look-in* also followed every fashionable fad, which in the 1970s included yo-yos and skateboarding. Interviews, picture stories and competitions were also featured, as well as pull-out posters of television, film and pop stars.

Smash Hits

Launched in 1978, you were A NOBODY if you didn't get a copy. This pop music bible aimed at teens and young adults was issued fortnightly. Parents found it a highly effective bargaining tool for getting homework done; 'do your fractions or *Smash Hits* goes in the budgie's cage'.

JACKIE

The market leader in magazines for teenage girls, the advice of Agony Aunts Cathy & Clare represented the only words of wisdom a girl needed. Spanning an incredible 29 years, *Jackie* is fondly remembered by many.

YOU KNOW YOU'RE A CHILD OF THE 1970s WHEN...

All the **clothes** you wore back then (and your **haircuts**) can now be found on humorous birthday cards.

You could always count on your best friend's mum to give you a glass of warm, **semi-flat Tizer**.

You remember a **peanut farmer** being elected president... and thinking the Americans couldn't get any more ludicrous than that.

You were genuinely **shocked** when you found out where pop group **10cc** got their name from.

QUIZ

1 Part of a famous family, which American singing brother and sister had their own TV show?

2 Playing the cabaret circuit and breaking into television in the 1970s, how are comedy duo Janette and Ian Tough better known?

3 Which comedy duo was responsible for the Phantom Raspberry Blower?

4 Regan and Carter featured in which TV cop show?

5 Which singing siblings had hits with 'We've Only Just Begun' and 'Superstar'?

6 Hosted by Derek Batey, which TV show was all about couples?

7 Who married his TV 'glamorous assistant' Anthea Redfern in 1973?

8 Which crime-fighting duo had a mate called Huggy Bear?

YOU KNOW YOU'RE A CHILD OF THE 1970s WHEN...

You thought you laughed out loud at **The Two Ronnies**. Now, seeing reruns of the show, you realise you must have been mistaken.

You sometimes get the urge to put your fingers in your **belt loops** and do the 'Tiger Feet' dance.

A rite of passage was heralded by changing from *Beezer* and *The Dandy* to *Cor!!* and *Whizzer and Chips*.

Being taken to a **Wimpy** bar was seen as a treat.

DO YOU REMEMBER...

Tubular Bells

Remember dancing around the school gym waving a chiffon scarf to this? Mike Oldfield's groundbreaking instrumental album that launched Virgin Records wasn't quite as good decades later, when we bought it on CD.

A Night at the Opera

The fourth studio album by the British rock band Queen, released in November 1975, this is arguably Queen's finest hour. 'Bohemian Rhapsody' and 'You're My Best Friend' are perhaps the two best-known tracks, but there's not a duff one among them. Not got it in your collection? Hit 'buy it now' pronto.

GREASE

The soundtrack to the movie of the same name, the album sky-rocketed to success in its wake. With several tracks making the charts, and the stage musical still doing the rounds today, copies of the album continue to sell as fast as 'Grease Lightning'.

If you're interested in finding out more about our books, find us on Facebook at **Summersdale Publishers** and follow us on Twitter at **@Summersdale**.

www.summersdale.com

THE WIRE

MICHAEL ANDERSON GODWIN
Date of Death (D.O.D.) 5 March 1989

Godwin was serving time for murder in a South Carolina jail after narrowly escaping the electric chair on appeal. Six years into his sentence, a routine check found him dead in his cell, sitting naked on his metal toilet with a badly burned mouth. It transpired that while trying to fix a pair of earphones attached to his TV, the convict had bitten into a live wire and was killed in his own electric chair.

INTRODUCTION

In the time it takes you to read this sentence, five people will have died somewhere in the world. They probably passed away quite peacefully in thankfully boring ways, but occasionally humans shuffle off this mortal coil in a more interesting fashion. This book contains a choice selection of particularly noteworthy deaths from around the globe, spanning the ancient world to the present day. Some of these exits serve as tragic warnings from beyond the grave, such as the sword swallower who took on a violin bow, and some are unbelievable accidents, like the farmer killed by her own sheep. And some are so shocking that they don't belong in the introduction. What they all have in common is that they are very, very unusual. Enter – if you dare! – the world of the dead.

UNUSUAL WAYS
TO DIE

History's Weirdest
DEATHS

James Proud

summersdale

UNUSUAL WAYS TO DIE

An Hachette UK Company
www.hachette.co.uk

Summersdale Publishers Ltd
Part of Octopus Publishing Group Limited
Carmelite House
50 Victoria Embankment
LONDON
EC4Y 0DZ
UK

www.summersdale.com

Printed and bound in the Czech Republic

ISBN: 978-1-78685-290-8

Substantial discounts on bulk quantities of Summersdale books are available to corporations, professional associations and other organisations. For details contact general enquiries by telephone: +44 (0) 1243 771107 or email: enquiries@summersdale.com.

TRAGICOMEDY

ALEX MITCHELL
D.O.D. 24 March 1975

Alex Mitchell was watching an episode of the comedy show *The Goodies* at home in Norfolk when a particularly funny sketch involving bagpipes sent him into a fit of hysterics. His wife didn't find it funny when he laughed himself into cardiac arrest, but she later sent a letter to the show to thank them for making her husband's final moments so amusing.

DID YOU KNOW?

Legend has it that the eccentric Scottish Royalist Thomas Urquhart died from a laughing fit in 1660 after hearing that Charles II had been restored to the throne.

DID YOU KNOW?

- *You are more likely to be killed by a cow, a champagne cork, a ballpoint pen, hot tap water, a vending machine or being left-handed than by a shark.*

- *More people die in the first week of the year than any other.*

- *People are most likely to die in the morning, around 11 a.m.*

- *Monday is the most common day to suffer a fatal heart attack.*

- *If you are over 60, you are more likely to die on your birthday than any other day. Nobody is sure why, but theories include the psychological effects of reaching a milestone and the dangers of overindulgence on the big day.*

SKY DIED

REGINALD CHUA

D.O.D. 25 MAY 2000

Three hundred passengers on a flight in the Philippines were terrorised by an armed man wearing a balaclava and swimming goggles who threatened to detonate a grenade unless they gave him money. The hijacker then told the pilot to fly at a lower altitude so that he could escape with the swag, and donned what appeared to be a home-made parachute. He was reluctant to jump, so one of the crew helped him on his way with a shove. The robber's body was found embedded in mud the next day, having fallen from 1,800 metres. His makeshift canopy had failed to open.

PAIN OF THRONES
Gyӧrgy Dózsa
D.O.D. 1514

Hungarian hero Dózsa was the leader of a failed peasant uprising against the ruling classes. After his defeat he was made an example of. A red-hot crown was forced on to his head, and he was tied to an iron throne, which was heated until his body started to cook. To add insult to injury, his fellow rebels were forced to eat the charred flesh from his bones before he died.

WATER WAY TO GO

JENNIFER STRANGE

D.O.D. 12 January 2007

Twenty-eight-year-old mother Jennifer Strange took part in a contest called 'Hold Your Wee for a Wii' on a live radio show to try to win a games console for her family. The winner would be the person who drank the most water without taking a leak. After drinking almost 9 litres in three hours, Strange complained of feeling ill and failed to win the contest. A few hours later, she collapsed and died of water intoxication.

TOXIC TOADS

UNIDENTIFIED

D.O.D. MARCH 2017

A man died after eating a highly poisonous species of toad caught from a reservoir near Daejeon in South Korea. The unidentified 57-year-old had been fishing with friends for bullfrogs, an edible delicacy, which he then took to a local restaurant for preparation. Unfortunately, bullfrogs look very similar to the Korean water toad, the skin of which contains a deadly poison, and he had caught both. After eating his dish of bullfrogs, he began vomiting violently, was taken to hospital and died early the next morning.

THE HUMAN OVEN

VLADIMIR LADYZHENSKIY
D.O.D. 7 August 2010

In Finland, sitting in saunas is a competitive sport. At the 2010 world championships in Heinola, two men were left sitting in the 110ºC heat: the home favourite and reigning champ Timo Kaukonen and Vladimir Ladyzhenskiy from Siberia. The Russian lasted the longest but the new champion was in no condition to celebrate, and both men passed out after suffering extensive burns. Kaukonen awoke from a coma several weeks later, but Ladyzhenskiy died as a result. It was the last ever such event.

A GAME OF TWO HALVES

BENA TSHADI FC

D.O.D. 25 October 1998

The football team Basanga were hosting Bena Tshadi in a match in the Democratic Republic of Congo. The score was 1–1 when a bolt of lightning struck the pitch, knocking the players off their feet. As the Basanga players slowly recovered, they realised that the entire away team had been killed, while they had survived unscathed. Local media speculated that witchcraft was to blame.

DID YOU KNOW?

- *Cotard's Delusion, or 'walking corpse syndrome', is a mental condition in which the patient believes they are dead.*

- *Botulinum Neurotoxin type H, similar to that used in Botox treatments, is so toxic that just 1.8 kilograms of it would be enough to kill every person on earth.*

- *Eighteen people died playing American football at US colleges during 1905.*

- *A storm of giant hailstones killed 246 people (plus 1,600 cattle and sheep) in Moradabad, India, in 1888.*

- *Devastating tornadoes caused four deaths in North Texas in March 2000. Juan Carlos Oseguera from Honduras ran for cover when the storm hit, but he was struck on the head by a hailstone the size of a cricket ball and died the next day.*

SUGARY GRAVE

NATASHA HARRIS
D.O.D. FEBRUARY 2010

A coroner in New Zealand found that a habit of drinking up to 10 litres of Coca-Cola a day was a 'substantial factor' in the premature death of Natasha Harris, who suffered a cardiac arrest at the age of 30. The coroner revealed that Harris would suffer withdrawal symptoms if she ran out of the drink, and that her teeth had fallen out as a result of her addiction. The amounts of caffeine and sugar Harris was reported to have been drinking daily were equivalent to downing ten cups of coffee and a whole bag of sugar.

In the eleventh century, the young King Edmund II ruled southern England in a fragile truce with the Viking King Canute. At least, he did for a few months – until he became one of history's most undignified murder victims. A traitorous nobleman called Eadric told his son to crawl into the cesspit underneath a privy (a medieval toilet) and wait for the king to do his business. When unsuspecting Edmund dropped his trousers, the youth stuck a sword into his bowels from below.

GOING UNDERGROUND

DANIEL JONES
D.O.D. 7 August 1997

One minute, you're happily digging a hole at the beach; the next, you've buried yourself alive. Daniel Jones was sitting at the bottom of the 8-feet-deep hole he had dug in the beach at Buxton, North Carolina, when his sandy excavations collapsed on top of him. Fellow beachgoers frantically tried to reach him, but to no avail. It took rescue workers with heavy equipment an hour to finally dig him out, but he had suffocated already.

I REST MY CASE

CLEMENT VALLANDIGHAM
D.O.D. 17 June 1871

Clement Vallandigham was a distinguished Ohio lawyer whose dedication to the job would be the end of him. In 1871 he defended a man accused of shooting someone dead during a card game, and he went to great lengths to get his man off the charge. Vallandigham suspected that the victim shot himself in the stomach when drawing his own weapon, and he conducted his own experiments to prove it. He demonstrated his theory to colleagues by drawing a gun from his own pocket, as the victim might have done, and pulling the trigger. Unfortunately, the gun was loaded and he shot himself in the stomach. Vallandigham's demonstration won the case, but he died the next day from his injuries.

SHOCK 'N' ROLL

LESLIE HARVEY
D.O.D. 3 May 1972

The Stone the Crows guitarist was playing a gig in Swansea when he touched an ungrounded microphone and was electrocuted. A roadie unplugged his guitar to try to save him, but it was too late and he collapsed onstage, dying later in hospital.

BULLETPROOF

ALEOBIGA ABERIMA
D.O.D. MARCH 2001

Aberima asked a local witch doctor in his native Ghana if he could cast a spell that would render him impervious to bullets. The witch doctor set to work – presumably safe in the knowledge that the spell would never be put to the test – and smeared a herbal lotion on the patient's skin over several days. Unfortunately for both of them, Aberima asked a friend to shoot him to test the spell. Surprisingly, it didn't work, and the doctor was almost beaten to death himself by angry villagers.

VEGGING OUT

BASIL BROWN
D.O.D. February 1974

Scientific adviser Basil Brown, from Surrey, was fanatical about his health. He began drinking a lot of carrot juice because he thought he was deficient in vitamin A – up to 4.5 litres of juice a day, topped up with vast amounts of vitamin pills. He drank so much carrot juice that his body couldn't process it, causing him to turn bright yellow and die of cirrhosis of the liver. A doctor had warned him that his liver was becoming enlarged, but, as the inquest was told, 'he had a low opinion of doctors'.

UNUSUAL CUSTOMS

- *The Yanomami people of the Amazon drink the cremated ashes of their dead with banana juice at funeral ceremonies.*

- *The Änga people of Papua New Guinea traditionally mummified their dead relatives by smoking them over a fire. They wore their fingers as jewellery.*

- *The Malagasy people of Madagascar exhume their dead every few years. The bodies are wrapped in fresh cloth, sprayed with perfume and wine, and then relatives dance with the bones of their ancestors.*

- *In Indonesia, the Batak people ritually dig up the bodies of their dead relatives, clean their bones and move them to a new burial site.*

- *The native people of the Philippines have many different funeral traditions. In Benguet province, dead bodies are blindfolded then propped up in a chair outside their house for a week before the funeral. The Ilongot people are buried sitting up. The Isneg people of Apayao bury their dead underneath their kitchens; while in the mountains of Sagada, the dead are put to rest in coffins hanging from cliffs.*

KNIGHTS OUT

PAUL ALLEN
D.O.D. 20 September 2007

Paul Allen, 54, was a history enthusiast who enjoyed military re-enactments. In 2007, he took part in a medieval jousting demonstration for the *Time Team* TV show, using light balsa wood lances for safety. As he rode into his adversary's lance, it shattered on impact with his shield as required, but a splinter flew through a slit in his helmet, penetrated his eye and lodged in his brain. He was taken to hospital but died a week later. Hundreds of people wearing historical costumes attended his funeral.

SMOKING IS BAD FOR YOU

GARY ALLEN BANNING
D.O.D. 28 FEBRUARY 2012

Forty-three-year-old Banning was at a friend's house in North Carolina when he picked up a jar of petrol from the kitchen and took a swig, mistaking the contents for a drink. He spat the fuel out in disgust, and went on with his evening. Sometime later, he decided to have a cigarette. As he lit up, he really lit up, as the gasoline residue on his clothes burst into flames. He was taken to hospital after firefighters responded to a call from a neighbour who detected the blaze, but he died the next day.

IT'S A GAS

JASON ACKERMAN AND SARA RYDMAN
D.O.D. 3 June 2006

Two students from Florida were found dead inside a giant helium balloon used to advertise an apartment complex. It appeared that Jason Ackerman and Sara Rydman had pulled the 8-foot balloon to the ground and crawled inside for a laugh. Helium gas makes your voice squeaky, but it also displaces oxygen in the bloodstream, so when the pair inhaled the amounts contained in the giant balloon, it caused them to lose consciousness and die as their brains were starved of oxygen.

KITCHEN NIGHTMARE

PHILLIP QUINN

D.O.D. 28 November 2004

Phillip Quinn, 24, of Washington, USA, was found dead in his static caravan with a shard of glass from a broken lava lamp stuck through his heart. Nobody else was present when he died, and his death was a mystery, until investigators concluded that Quinn had heated the lava lamp on a cooker. The heat had caused such pressure in the lamp that it violently exploded, sending shards of glass into Quinn's chest. The reasoning behind the risky experiment remains unknown.

PLAYING DEAD

BRANDON LEE
D.O.D. 31 MARCH 1993

Actor Brandon Lee, the son of martial arts legend Bruce, was filming a scene for *The Crow* in which his character is shot at from close range. Blank cartridges, with powder but no bullets, were required for authenticity. As the gun was 'fired', Lee crumpled to the floor, fatally wounded in the stomach by a real bullet that had remained in the gun from a previous scene – the blank propelled that bullet out of the barrel and into Lee.

GIVEN A GRILLING

SAINT LAWRENCE
D.O.D. 10 August 258

Saint Lawrence was a clergyman in Rome, during the third century, who met his death after refusing to give up the treasures of his church to the authorities. The Roman prefect was so enraged by Lawrence's resistance that he had him tied to a giant gridiron and roasted over a fire. The story goes that when his torturers asked if he had suffered enough, Lawrence said, 'Turn me over. I'm well done!' Suitably, he is the patron saint of chefs and comedians to this day.

RISQUÉ BUSINESS

PAUL COWLEY AND KIM FONTANA
D.O.D. 3 March 2002

An amorous couple were on a night out in Sheffield when their urges got the better of them, and they decided to get down to it in the middle of a public road. A passing off-duty paramedic stopped to tell them of the danger they were in, but they went on with their courting – until an approaching bus driver mistook the pair for 'a bag of rubbish' in the dim light. The bus failed to take avoiding action, and they were both killed instantly.

HUNGRY HOGS

TERRY GARNER
D.O.D. 26 September 2012

Terry Garner was an Oregon pig farmer who owned some gigantic specimens weighing as much as 320 kilograms. On the day he died, he went to feed the animals as usual, and never came back. When a relative went to the pigpen to look for Garner, what he found chilled his blood. Strewn amongst the snuffling sows were Garner's personal items, a pair of dentures and what remained of the man himself – which wasn't much. Not even enough, in fact, to determine a cause of death. All we know is that the 69-year-old farmer was eaten by his own pigs.

FIGHTING BLIND

JOHN OF BOHEMIA
D.O.D. 26 AUGUST 1346

King John I of Bohemia had been blind for several years before he met his end at the Battle of Crécy. He was determined not to be left out of the fun, so he ordered his men to tie their horses to his own, in order that he could ride into battle with them. They all died at the hands of the English and were found still tied together the next morning.

THE EMPEROR'S NEW PILLS

QIN SHI HUANG
D.O.D. 210 BCE

Huang was the first emperor of China, the man famous for building the Great Wall and being buried with thousands of terracotta warriors. He became paranoid about death after surviving three assassination attempts, and sought out herbs and potions from far and wide in his search for a life-giving elixir. One such 'cure' was mercury pills, a surprisingly common treatment at the time. It's unclear why Huang thought eating the toxic metal would be a good idea – but it wasn't, and he fatally poisoned himself.

DID YOU KNOW?

- *In 897, Pope Stephen VI exhumed his penultimate predecessor, Formosus, and put him on trial for being a bad pope. He was found guilty.*

- *In 1920, 10,000 people attended the funeral of a canary called Jimmy in Newark, New Jersey.*

- *It is legal to marry a dead person in France – if the wedding was planned before their death.*

- *Before he became the president of the USA in 1885, Grover Cleveland acted as executioner as part of his duties while sheriff of Erie County, and hanged two people.*

DANCE TILL YOU DROP

HOMER MOREHOUSE
D.O.D. 14 April 1923

In the 1920s, a new fad of dance marathons took hold in the USA. Couples would dance for as long as they could, with only short breaks, in order to remain the last dancers standing and claim a prize. Some competitions lasted for several weeks at a time. One of several casualties was 27-year-old Homer Morehouse of New York, who dropped down dead from heart failure upon leaving the dance floor after 87 hours of jiving.

CASKET FALL

HENRY TAYLOR
D.O.D. 19 October 1872

An extra death haunted a funeral in a London cemetery when one of the pall-bearers, 60-year-old Henry Taylor, tripped on a gravestone and fell as the coffin was transported along a narrow path towards the grave. His fellow coffin carriers lost control of the casket and dropped it on top of him. After some confusion, the burial continued as planned while Taylor was taken to hospital, but he died of his injuries a few days later.

DISAPPEARING ACT

CHARLES ROWAN
D.O.D. 1930

The South African Charles Rowan performed as Karr the Magician. One of his tricks was to escape from a straitjacket as a car accelerated towards him. His last performance was in Springfontein in front of a large crowd. He managed to wriggle free from the jacket with seconds to spare, which unfortunately wasn't enough. The car struck him and 'almost severed' his right leg, and he quickly succumbed to his injuries.

MAKING A SPLASH

CHARLES STEPHENS
D.O.D. 11 July 1920

Charles Stephens, a 58-year-old English barber and amateur daredevil, went over Niagara Falls in a barrel in 1920. He optimistically wanted to remain upright, so he installed straps for his arms and tied an anvil to his feet for ballast. Stephens plunged into the pool at the bottom of the falls with such force that the anvil smashed through the bottom of the barrel and took the barber with it, leaving only his right arm to be found.

NIAGARA FAIL

GEORGE A. STATHAKIS
D.O.D. 5 July 1930

When George A. Stathakis plunged over Niagara Falls in a home-made barrel, the 46-year-old chef from New York was accompanied for unknown reasons by his pet turtle Sonny. His custom barrel was ten feet long, reinforced with steel, and said to weigh a ton. Its strength ensured that Stathakis survived the 50-metre drop, but the heavy barrel didn't emerge from the maelstrom until the next morning, by which time he had suffocated. Incredibly, Sonny is reported to have survived the fall.

ISN'T IT IRONIC

Bobby Leach
D.O.D. April 1926

Bobby Leach was an English stuntman who went over Niagara Falls in a barrel in July 1911. But the fall didn't kill him (though it took six months for him to recover from his injuries), and he became only the second person to survive the trip. He went on to perform other death-defying feats, including several failed attempts at swimming the Niagara rapids, and toured the world regaling audiences with the tales of his escapades. In 1926, Leach's luck ran out after slipping on a banana skin and breaking his leg in New Zealand. The injury became infected and he died two months later.

BAD AIM

KAREL SOUCEK
D.O.D. 20 JANUARY 1985

In 1984, Canadian Karel Soucek survived going over Niagara Falls in a barrel unscathed. So why is he in this book? The following year, Soucek planned a stunt where he would be nailed into another barrel and dropped from 180 feet into a water tank just 12 feet wide. As the barrel plunged towards the ground, it spun off target and bounced off the side of the tank on to the ground. The 45,000-strong crowd applauded the stunt, but realised that things had not gone to plan when paramedics rushed on to the scene and carried the daredevil away. Soucek suffered terrible crush injuries and a fractured skull, from which he did not recover.

MAD
SCIENTIST
JESSE WILLIAM LAZEAR
D.O.D. September 1900

Scientist Jesse William Lazear worked at a US Army barracks in Cuba, where he was part of a team investigating the deadly yellow fever that its troops were suffering from. He was so determined to prove his theory that mosquitoes were responsible for the illness that he deliberately allowed the bugs to bite him in order to study the disease in his own body. Sure enough, he soon contracted yellow fever, triumphantly proving his theory – but bringing about his own death within a couple of weeks.

OLIVE
TWIST

SHERWOOD ANDERSON
D.O.D. 8 March 1941

The American novelist Sherwood Anderson committed the grave error of making a meal of a cocktail on board a ship bound for South America. He swallowed an 8-centimetre toothpick from an olive while drinking a Martini, his favourite drink. He developed terrible stomach pains, and died in Panama of peritonitis.

DEAD LEG

SIR ARTHUR ASTON
D.O.D. 10 SEPTEMBER 1649

During the invasion of Ireland in the English Civil War, Oliver Cromwell's Roundhead forces laid siege to Drogheda. The town was held by Royalist troops under the command of Sir Arthur Aston, who had lost a leg earlier in the campaign and was rumoured to keep gold coins in the replacement wooden limb. Cromwell offered to let Aston surrender, but the veteran refused. When the Roundheads finally breached the town walls and found Aston, they seized his wooden leg and 'beat his brains out' with it.

LAVA LEAP

Empedocles was a Greek philosopher from the island of Sicily. He believed that death was caused by the cooling of the blood; therefore it followed that by jumping into the active volcanic crater of Mount Etna you would become a god and live for ever. It's not certain whether Empedocles was successful, but he certainly moved on from this life in one way or another.

UNLUCKY LETTER

THAN SINGH
D.O.D. June 2010

Seventy-year-old Than Singh of India was surprised to receive a letter from a local crematorium, as none of his family or friends had died recently. When he opened it, he was shocked to see that it was a receipt for his own cremation – so shocked, in fact, that he suffered a heart attack and died later in hospital. When Singh was cremated for real, in the very same crematorium, his family received another receipt, with the same serial number.

PIPE DRAMA

RAY LANGSTON
D.O.D. September 1996

Ray Langston's day went from bad to really, really bad after he dropped his car keys down a drain outside his brother's house in Detroit, Michigan. The 41-year-old managed to hoist open the 60-kilo drain cover using a coat hanger, and squeezed his body into the 45-centimetre-wide hole. But as he stretched for his keys, he fell down the pipe, pinning himself head first in the sewer water. Despite his brother's efforts to shift him, Ray was stuck fast, and he drowned in 2 feet of water.

THE HYPOCHONDRIAC

MOLIÈRE
D.O.D. 17 FEBRUARY 1673

The French playwright and actor Molière suffered from tuberculosis for many years, and, unsurprisingly, it caused his death. More surprising were the time and place of his demise. He collapsed in a bloody coughing fit onstage during a performance of *The Imaginary Invalid*, a new play he had written, in which he played a hypochondriac constantly suffering from 'illness'. Molière managed to complete the show, but died later that day.

DID YOU KNOW?

- *It's estimated that 50,000 people were burned as witches in Europe between 1450 and 1750, and 20 per cent of them were men.*

- *Powder made by grinding up ancient Egyptian mummies became a popular medicine in Europe in the sixteenth century and was still in use as late as the twentieth century.*

- *In 1900, the average global life expectancy was 31 years.*

- *A small number of people still die of the Black Death every year in the USA.*

- *The last execution by guillotine in France took place in 1977.*

FEEDING TIME

NORDIN MONTONG

D.O.D. 13 November 2008

A Malaysian cleaner who worked at Singapore Zoo gave up his life in a bizarre fashion when he jumped into an enclosure containing three gigantic white tigers. The big cats immediately started to play with their new toy, who had only a bucket and broom for protection. By the time the tigers were distracted by keepers, they had inflicted fatal injuries.

PLANT POWER

DAVID GRUNDMAN

D.O.D. 1982

David Grundman and his friend James Suchochi were playing around with guns in the desert in Arizona, taking potshots at the large saguaro cacti that grow in the area, a practice known as 'cactus plugging'. Grundman took aim at one old specimen that stood more than 7 metres high, and blew a heavy branch off with his first shot. He was standing too close, however, and the spiky limb crushed him to death.

PAIN IN THE NECK

PATRICK MULRANEY
D.O.D. 29 June 1891

Mulraney was a circus juggler and sword swallower who set aside his swords during a performance in Columbus, Ohio, and endeavoured to swallow a violin bow instead. After trying and failing twice on account of the pain, he began to cough up blood in front of the horrified audience. Mulraney continued to suffer in this fashion until the next morning, when he died.

TIGHT SPOT

JOHN JONES
D.O.D. 25 NOVEMBER 2009

John Jones was part of a group of cavers crawling through underground tunnels at a popular site in Utah. He branched off on his own and squeezed head-first through a downward-sloping passage just 45 by 25 centimetres. It was a dead end, but as he tried to back out, Jones realised he was stuck fast. His friends tried and failed to shift him, and despite the efforts of 50 rescue workers he remained trapped 38 metres below ground. After 28 hours, Jones lost consciousness, and his rescuers had to concede defeat. His body was never recovered, and the cave was permanently sealed.

BUNGEE BUNGLE

MICHAEL LUSH
D.O.D. 13 November 1986

In the 1980s, the BBC programme *The Late, Late Breakfast Show* enlisted and trained members of the public to perform genuinely dangerous stunts live on TV. Michael Lush, a builder, was one of those chosen. He was to escape from a box suspended by a crane 36 metres above the ground before it 'exploded' then jump to the ground on a bungee rope. During rehearsals, he managed to escape from the box but fell to his death when the rope came loose. The series was cancelled as a result of the tragedy.

WORK SUCKS

Ravi Subramanian
D.O.D. 16 December 2015

The crew of Air India flight 619 from Mumbai to Hyderabad were running late due to a scheduling clash. They rushed to the cockpit and prepared for take-off. In his haste to get going, the co-pilot mistook a gesture from the ground crew for a thumbs-up all-clear signal, and started the engine while someone was still working under the plane. Technician Ravi Subramanian was sucked into the jet engine's turbine and obliterated.

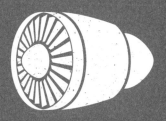

DEEP FREEZE

CHELSEA AKE-SALVACION
D.O.D. 20 October 2015

Whole-body cryotherapy involves exposing the body to extremely cold air (below −100°C) in liquid nitrogen tanks for up to 4 minutes at a time. The process is supposed to burn calories, reduce inflammation and prevent ageing. Las Vegas cryotherapist Chelsea Ake-Salvacion texted her boyfriend while working late one evening to say that she was going to use one of the pods. He never heard from her again. The next morning, colleagues found her frozen solid at the bottom of the tank. It's thought that Ake-Salvacion died from asphyxiation due to inhaling the noxious gas produced by the liquid nitrogen.

RUN THROUGH

JON DESBOROUGH
D.O.D. 10 JUNE 1999

Pupils at a Liverpool school were being shown how to throw the javelin in a PE class. The teacher, Jon Desborough, demonstrated how to safely retrieve the javelin from the field, but as he reached for a spear sticking out of the ground, he slipped on the grass and fell on to the blunt end of the shaft. It passed through his eye socket and into his skull. Desborough was able to calmly tell his pupils to walk away and get help, but he fell into a coma and died three weeks later due to complications from his injury.

THE FINAL COUNTDOWN

UNIDENTIFIED TERRORISTS

D.O.D. 5 September 1999

In 1999, a gang of Palestinian terrorists were planning twin bomb attacks on buses in two Israeli cities. One group would build the bombs in Palestinian territory, and another group was tasked with planting them on buses in Israel. What neither realised was that while the timed devices were set to Palestinian summertime, clocks in Israel – and the courier's watches – had already been switched to standard time. The bombs exploded as programmed, but an hour too early for the terrorists. They were still en route to the bus stations, and three out of the four plotters were killed.

BEWARE OF THE BIRD

PHILLIP MCCLEAN
D.O.D. 6 April 1926

The cassowary is a large flightless bird of Australasia – with a fearsome reputation. It will use its powerful legs and razor-sharp talons to kick at anything it considers a threat, including humans. In 1926 in North Queensland, 16-year-old Phillip McClean came across a cassowary in his garden and decided to attack it with a club. The bird lashed out and Phillip tripped and fell, whereupon the cassowary kicked him in the neck and severed an artery. He bled to death, becoming one of the few people ever to be killed by a bird.

FAULTY LOGIC

KURT GÖDEL
D.O.D. 14 JANUARY 1978

Austrian American Kurt Gödel was a world-famous mathematician and logical philosopher. As he grew older, he began to suffer from paranoid delusions and developed an illogical fear of being poisoned, only eating food that had been prepared by his wife, Adele. When, in his seventies, his wife was hospitalised, Gödel refused to eat anything provided by anybody else. Unfortunately, Adele was in hospital for so long that by the time she returned, Gödel weighed only 30 kilograms. He was admitted to hospital, but died two weeks later of malnutrition and exhaustion.

DIE DIVE

IVAN LESTER MCGUIRE
D.O.D. 2 April 1988

He was an experienced skydiver with hundreds of jumps under his belt, but Ivan Lester McGuire made one jump too many. On the day in question, he was videoing a student, with a helmet camera and recording equipment in his backpack – this was way back in 1988. The recovered footage shows McGuire jumping from the plane, but his parachute never opens... because there was no parachute – he had forgotten to pack one. It's speculated that a combination of tiredness and confusion caused by the weight of the camera equipment in his backpack led to the fatal error.

HEAVY METAL

In the twelfth century, during the Third Crusade, the King of Germany and Holy Roman Emperor Frederick I led an army to recapture Jerusalem from the Muslim leader Saladin. His mighty forces swept aside all before them, until they came to the River Saleph (in present-day Turkey). As his horse waded across, Frederick I fell into the water and drowned, weighed down by his armour. His troops' participation in the Crusade ended with his death and the Third Crusade failed to capture the holy city.

TENNIS FALL

DICK WERTHEIM
D.O.D. 15 September 1983

During the boys' final at the 1983 US Open, a young Stefan Edberg of Sweden sent down a serve that struck line judge Dick Wertheim so hard in the groin that he fell from his chair and struck his head on the hard court surface. He suffered brain damage and died a week later. Edberg would go on to win the men's championships twice.

LOST
HIS HEAD

TERRY KATH
D.O.D. 23 JANUARY 1978

Terry Kath, the guitarist with rock band Chicago, was at a friend's party in Los Angeles. At the end of the evening, gun nut Kath started to play with a couple of firearms he had with him, putting an empty pistol to his head and playing Russian roulette. When he picked up a 9-mm automatic, his friend told him to be careful. 'Don't worry, it's not loaded,' he said, showing an empty magazine. Kath put the barrel to his head and pulled the trigger. Unfortunately, there was a bullet already in the chamber and he died instantly.

YOU SWING ME RIGHT ROUND...

WILLIAM SNYDER
D.O.D. January 1854

If you suffer from coulrophobia (an irrational fear of clowns), look away now. According to his intriguing death certificate, 13-year-old William Snyder of Cincinnati, Ohio, died in 1854 after 'being swung around by the heels by a circus clown'. The exact cause of death – whether he died of sheer fright, or when the clown let go mid-swing – is not recorded.

CRIMINAL DAMAGE

SANTIAGO ALVARADO
D.O.D. 3 February 1997

Twenty-five-year-old Santiago Alvarado died in the process of burgling a bike shop in Lompoc, California. It appeared that he fell as he tried to enter the shop through the roof at night. As he hit the floor, the torch held in his mouth was driven back into his throat with such force that it broke his neck.

ALCOHOL ABUSE

GEORGE PLANTAGENET
D.O.D. 18 February 1478

George Plantagenet, duke of Clarence, took part in more than one rebellion against his brother, King Edward IV, and was eventually convicted of treason. He was executed, but in a more imaginative – and expensive – fashion than was normal at the time. He was drowned in a barrel of malmsey wine, reportedly at his own request.

UNUSUAL METHODS OF EXECUTION

- **Crushed by elephant** *(southern Asia) – a practice that continued until the nineteenth century.*

- **The brazen bull** *(ancient Greece) – victims were cooked alive inside a bronze bull, their screams issuing from its mouth.*

- **Rat torture** *(Europe) – during the sixteenth century, hungry rats were placed on the victim's belly, under an upturned bucket upon which red-hot coals were piled (to force the rats to gnaw their way away from the heat).*

- **Death by a thousand cuts** *(China) – victims were tied up in public and sliced up slowly until they died, a custom that was finally outlawed in 1905.*

DANCE MACABRE

JEAN-BAPTISTE LULLY
D.O.D. 22 MARCH 1687

Lully was a renowned composer and ballet dancer at the court of the French King Louis XIV. He was leading a performance in a Paris church when enthusiastic conducting led him to crush his toe with the long stick he used to keep rhythm with the music. He contracted gangrene of the foot, possibly because he refused to give up dancing, and court doctors recommended amputation. The keen dancer refused treatment, and it proved to be the death of him.

FROZEN CHICKEN

FRANCIS BACON
D.O.D. 9 April 1626

The renowned Elizabethan polymath, writer and philosopher of science liked to carry out his own experiments. One winter, Bacon was travelling through a snowy London when he had an idea: why not use the cold white stuff to preserve meat? He broke from his journey, found a chicken and stuffed the carcass full of snow in an early attempt at refrigeration. Unfortunately, his chilly mission led him to contract a fatal bout of pneumonia.

UNLUCKY STARS

MARC AARONSON
D.O.D. 30 April 1987

Aaronson was a noted astronomer who observed the night sky through a giant telescope with a rotating dome in Tucson, Arizona. The revolving roof would automatically come to a stop when workers opened the door to check the weather. Aaronson died after popping outside one night just as the 500-ton dome was coasting to a halt. A ladder hanging from it smashed into the open door, which crushed him to death.

DENTAL HEALTH

Agathocles was an ambitious potter who became a soldier, married into wealth and then seized power by force after several attempts. The self-styled King of Sicily was a cruel ruler who was not well liked, and he met his end after using a toothpick that one of his enemies had dipped in poison. The toxin rendered him paralysed but alive, and it was in that state that he was laid on his burning funeral pyre.

BROLLY UNLUCKY

GEORGI MARKOV
D.O.D. 11 SEPTEMBER 1978

Georgi Markov was a dissident writer from communist Bulgaria who defected to the West in the late 1960s. Ten years later, he was waiting for a bus on London's Waterloo Bridge when he felt a sharp pain in his leg. He looked around and saw a man running away with an umbrella. Later that day Markov developed a fever, and four days later he was dead. Investigations concluded that the assassin had used a modified umbrella to inject a tiny pellet containing the deadly poison ricin, for which there is no known antidote.

BEARING
A GRUDGE

JÖRG JENATSCH
D.O.D. 24 January 1639

Jörg Jenatsch was a Swiss politician who made many enemies during the Thirty Years War. His deeds came back to haunt him when he attended a party during carnival season in the town of Chur. A group of men disguised in costumes entered the event, and a mysterious assassin dressed as a bear hacked Jenatsch to death with an axe.

REBEL
ROBOT

Robert Williams
D.O.D. 25 January 1979

Robert Williams was working at a Ford Motor factory in Michigan when he was fatally struck in the head by the arm of a one-ton robot carrying car parts. Williams was hit while climbing a rack of metal castings after the machine had malfunctioned. His was the first recorded death by robot – and it would not be the last...

SWEET KISS OF...

FRANK HAYES
D.O.D. 4 JUNE 1923

Part-time jockey Frank Hayes was riding a 20–1-shot horse called Sweet Kiss in a steeplechase in New York state when he slumped over in the middle of the race. He had suffered a fatal heart attack but somehow remained in the saddle as Sweet Kiss jumped the remaining fences undeterred and won the race by a head. Hayes had secured his first-ever victory, but he was dead before he crossed the finish line, becoming the only known jockey to win a race after death.

EASY TIGER

HANNAH TWYNNOY
D.O.D. 23 October 1703

Hannah Twynnoy was a barmaid at the White Lion pub in Malmesbury, Wiltshire, when a travelling zoo featuring a caged tiger came to town. She was fascinated by the tiger and kept teasing it, despite being repeatedly warned of the danger. One day while she was taunting it, it escaped its enclosure and mauled her to death. Twynnoy was surely the first person to be killed by a tiger in Britain. The incident is recorded on her gravestone:

*In bloom of life
She's snatch'd from hence,
She had not room
To make defence;
For Tyger fierce
Took life away,
And here she lies
In a bed of Clay,
Until the Resurrection Day.*

PAIN IN THE LEG

Sigurd the Mighty, the Earl of Orkney, was killed by an enemy from beyond the grave. After defeating fellow nobleman Máel Brigte in battle, he tied his foe's decapitated head to his horse as a trophy of war. While Sigurd was riding home victorious, he grazed his leg on Brigte's teeth as he spurred his horse, inflicting a minor wound that eventually caused a fatal infection.

DID YOU KNOW?

- *When William the Conqueror died in 1087, his obese body became bloated with gas because the burial was delayed. His body burst when monks tried to fit the swollen corpse into a coffin, filling the church with a putrid stench.*

- *In 1567, Hans Steininger, the mayor of Braunau, Austria, died after tripping over his magnificent six-foot beard. He usually rolled it up to keep it out of the way, but one day a fire broke out, and in his hurry to escape he tripped over his facial hair and broke his neck. Steininger's beard is still on display in the town today.*

- *In January 1570, James Stewart, 1st Earl of Moray, was killed with a carbine (a type of early rifle) in the first successful assassination by firearm.*

- *In 1771, the renowned glutton King Adolf Frederick of Sweden died after eating a royal feast consisting of lobster, caviar, sauerkraut and herring, washed down with champagne and topped off with 14 Swedish pastries. He is thought to have died from a stroke.*

FASHION VICTIM

MARTHA MANSFIELD
D.O.D. 30 NOVEMBER 1923

Martha Mansfield, a promising young film actress, retired to a car with friends during a break in filming the American Civil War drama *The Warrens of Virginia*. Someone in the vehicle lit a match, and the heavy period dress Mansfield was wearing went up in flames. Cast and crew tried to save her, but they could not put the fire out in time and she suffered substantial burns, dying less than 24 hours later.

MONKEY BUSINESS

ALEXANDER OF GREECE
D.O.D. 25 October 1920

A healthy 27-year-old monarch, King Alexander of Greece had only reigned for three years when he was fatally injured by a pet monkey in the gardens of the royal palace in Athens. While trying to save one monkey from the jaws of his pet wolfhound, Alexander was bitten on the calf by another. The wound became infected and he contracted blood poisoning, which resulted in his death three weeks after the attack.

BALL BOY

ALAN FISH

D.O.D. 20 May 1970

Fourteen-year-old baseball fan Alan Fish was at Dodger Stadium in Los Angeles watching the home team play the San Francisco Giants, when the Dodgers' Manny Mota hit the ball into the stands, something that normally happens a few times every game. The ball caught Fish unawares and he was struck hard on the temple, but he appeared to be OK after some aspirin and he went home with his family. Four days later he died from the injury, becoming the first and the only spectator to die after being hit by the ball at a Major League Baseball game.

DID YOU KNOW?

Ray Chapman of the Cleveland Indians is the only player to have been killed by the ball during a Major League Baseball game. In 1920, pitcher Carl Mays of the New York Yankees threw a deliberate 'beanball' at Chapman's head so hard that his skull was fractured.

UDDER TERROR

João Maria de Souza
D.O.D. 11 July 2013

João Maria de Souza was in bed with his wife in the Brazilian town of Caratinga when a cow fell through their bedroom ceiling, landing on top of him and narrowly missing his wife. The one-ton animal had wandered on to the house from the hill behind and proved too heavy for the asbestos roof. De Souza was taken to hospital with serious internal injuries and died a day later.

THE FIRST OF MANY

MARY WARD
D.O.D. 31 August 1869

The Irish astronomer Mary Ward was riding in an early steam-powered car (built by her cousins) when she was thrown from the unwieldy contraption as it navigated a corner and crushed under the wheels. The 42-year-old's untimely demise was the first recorded death from an automobile accident.

DID YOU KNOW?

Henry H. Bliss was the first person to be killed by a car in the USA. He was struck by an electric taxi in New York City in 1899.

LOOK BOTH WAYS

Bridget Driscoll
D.O.D. 17 August 1896

Bridget Driscoll, 43, became the first pedestrian to die in a motor accident in the UK when she was knocked down by a car from the Anglo-French Motor Carriage Company while crossing the road in Crystal Palace, London. The early car was travelling at no more than 5 miles per hour, because that was as fast as it could go. The coroner said that he hoped such a thing would never happen again.

DEATH FROM ABOVE

AESCHYLUS
D.O.D. c. 450 BCE

The ancient Greek Aeschylus is one of the very few people in history to have been killed by a tortoise. The celebrated Athenian playwright had heard a prophecy that he would be killed by a 'falling house', and therefore spent most of his time outdoors. One day while walking under a clear sky, an eagle carrying a tortoise flew overhead. In an attempt to crack the reptile's shell, the bird dropped the tortoise on to the head of unsuspecting Aeschylus – and cracked his skull in the process.

BAD PUBLICITY

Jintaro Itoh
D.O.D. 17 September 1979

Businessman Jintaro Itoh was thinking of running for office in the Japanese general election, and he planned a risky PR stunt to gain sympathy from the public. He was to stab himself in the leg outside his home in a fake robbery then declare his candidacy as a hero from his hospital bed. When Itoh jabbed the knife into his thigh, he severed an artery and bled to death on the street.

OLD SOULS

LUANG PHO DAENG
D.O.D. 1973

When Thai Buddhist monk Luang Pho Daeng knew he would soon die, he decided to become a spiritual example to others. He began meditating and undertook a strict starvation diet to dry his body out, effectively mummifying himself before death. When he finally died – while meditating – he was preserved sitting in the lotus position, and he has been on display in the Wat Khunaram temple in Koh Samui ever since.

DID YOU KNOW?

The Russian writer Nikolai Gogol became increasingly eccentric in later life. The author of *Dead Souls* and *The Government Inspector* grew so delirious with obsessive prayer and religious fasting that he died of hunger in 1852 at the age of 42, having burned a manuscript he had been working on for five years.

SIX
FEET UNDER

JOE BURRUS
D.O.D. 31 OCTOBER 1990

American magician Joe Burrus planned to
escape being buried alive in a tribute to
Harry Houdini. He had achieved the feat a
year previously, but this time he went one
step further by using cement instead of soil.
The event took place on Halloween at an
amusement park in Fresno, California, before
an excited crowd. Burrus was handcuffed,
chained and placed in a transparent coffin
that was lowered into a freshly dug grave.
As the cement was poured in, witnesses
heard a muffled crack as the plastic coffin
broke under the weight, and Burrus was
crushed to death.

UNUSUAL BURIALS

- *When horror film legend Bela Lugosi died in 1956, he was buried in full Dracula costume.*

- *In 1977, the Texan socialite Sandra West was buried behind the wheel of her Ferrari 330 in a San Antonio cemetery.*

- *In 1992, some of the ashes of Star Trek creator Gene Roddenberry were taken into space on a space shuttle and returned to earth. Then in 1997, a portion of his ashes was launched from a rocket to orbit around the earth.*

- *In 2008, the ashes of Fredric J. Baur of Cincinnati were buried in a Pringles tube – he had designed the packaging in the 1960s.*

- *In 2014, Billy Standley of Ohio was buried on the back of his 1967 Harley-Davidson motorcycle. His embalmed body was propped up on the seat inside a transparent coffin.*

- *The ashes of Italian tycoon Renato Bialetti, who popularised the Moka stove-top coffee maker, were interred in a giant version of his iconic coffee pot in 2016.*

HEY PRESTO?

GILBERT GENESTA

D.O.D. 9 November 1930

Gilbert Genesta was a magician from Kentucky who regularly performed the famous milk-churn escape trick. He would lower himself into a container filled to the brim with water and secured with six padlocks, leaving him 2 minutes to escape before he drowned. One night, Genesta failed to appear in time and began banging frantically to be freed. By the time helpers had forced it open, Genesta was unconscious, and he died later in hospital. The secret of the trick was a fake lid that Genesta could easily lift off, without having to undo any padlocks, when hidden from view behind a curtain. What the magician didn't know was that the milk can had been dropped by stagehands earlier in the day. The accident had damaged the fake lid, jamming it shut for real.

YOU'RE FIRED

WILLIAM ELLSWORTH ROBINSON
D.O.D. 24 MARCH 1918

The signature trick of the illusionist William Ellsworth Robinson, who performed as Chung Ling Soo, was to catch the bullets fired from two guns – with fake barrels – in his teeth. Onstage in London one night, he fell to the floor when the guns were fired, crying, 'I've been shot! Lower the curtain!' He died the next day. Robinson hadn't cleaned the guns properly, and powder build-up in the fake barrels had ignited and fired real bullets.

DEAD LINE

JASON FINDLEY
D.O.D. 21 May 1985

Seventeen-year-old Jason Findley was found dead lying next to the telephone in his bedroom in New Jersey. His death was a mystery for months, until it was revealed that he had died from a lightning strike, despite the lack of visible burns on his body or damage in his room. The lightning had struck the phone line outside the house and delivered a fatal shock to his brain via the telephone receiver without leaving even a trace on the line.

PROFESSIONAL PRIDE

AMERICO SBIGOLI
D.O.D. January 1822

The Italian tenor Americo Sbigoli died during the performance of a Pacini opera. In attempting to match the first – more powerful – tenor, Sbigoli sang so hard that he burst a blood vessel in his neck and died shortly afterwards.

BIRDMAN

Franz Reichelt
D.O.D. 4 February 1912

Franz Reichelt of Austria believed he could fly. He designed a wing-like parachute suit and decided to test it from the Eiffel Tower in Paris. He secured permission to test his wingsuit on a dummy, but at the last moment decided to take the flight himself. After strapping the parachute to his limbs, he stepped off the edge and plummeted 57 metres to his death.

SILLY SAUSAGE

WALTER EAGLE TAIL
D.O.D. 4 JULY 2014

Forty-seven-year-old Walter Eagle Tail bit off more than he could chew when taking part in an Independence Day hot-dog-eating contest in South Dakota. In his frantic attempt to chow down more dogs than the other competitors, the speed-eating athlete stuffed too much into his mouth, choked and suffocated before paramedics could save him.

A BUG'S DEATH

EDWARD ARCHBOLD
D.O.D. 5 October 2012

A Florida reptile shop held a contest in which people competed to eat the most creepy-crawlies in order to win a python. Contestants struggled to chew through piles of cockroaches and worms, but Edward Archbold forced down the most bugs and emerged as the winner. He was unable to claim his prize, however, as he began to vomit, collapsed and died of suffocation after his airway became blocked with 'arthropod body parts'.

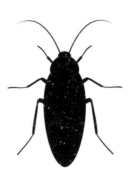

DID YOU KNOW?

- *In January 1919, a giant tank of molasses exploded in Boston, Massachusetts. The sticky tidal wave tore down buildings and killed 21 people.*

- *Hundreds of Indian children died every year after eating lychees, until in 2017 it was discovered that the popular fruit contains a toxin that is dangerous for small children to consume on an empty stomach.*

- *Several South Koreans have died while trying to eat live octopus. Problems occur when the creature's suckers stick in the throat while being swallowed.*

- *Kites annually kill several people in India – they are often garrotted by kite strings that have been coated with glass in the sport of kite-fighting.*

- *In 2009, businessman Jimi Heselden, who had made a fortune from safety barriers, bought the company that manufactures Segway scooters. A year later, he was riding one around his Yorkshire estate when he apparently lost control and rolled 12 metres over a cliff into a river. He was pronounced dead at the scene.*

DRINKY-POO

MICHAEL WARNER
D.O.D. 21 May 2004

Michael Warner of Texas died after a sherry enema. A 58-year-old alcoholic unable to swallow liquids, Warner got his wife to administer his booze from the wrong end, resulting in a blood alcohol level six times the drink-driving limit in Texas, and fatal alcohol poisoning. According to the police, the danger of such a procedure is that the body will continue to absorb alcohol even after the person loses consciousness. Warner's wife said her husband often took alcohol in such a manner. She was accused of negligent homicide for helping Warner with the procedure, but the charges were eventually dropped.

WATCH THIS

GARRY HOY
D.O.D. 9 July 1993

Garry Hoy was a lawyer at a leading Canadian law firm, based in a 56-storey skyscraper in downtown Toronto with impressive floor-to-ceiling glass windows. One evening, Hoy deployed his party trick while playing host to a group of young lawyers, shoving his body against the windows to demonstrate their strength. He took a run-up and threw his body at the glass, expecting to bounce off as usual. Unfortunately, the window gave way and the guests watched in horror as Hoy disappeared into the street below from the twenty-fourth floor.

GAME OF DEATH

Mr Hsieh
D.O.D. 8 January 2015

A certain Mr Hsieh had settled in for another long session playing online computer games at a Taiwanese internet cafe. Three days later, his fellow gamers noticed him slumped over his keyboard, but this was not unusual – they assumed he was just taking a rest. When staff finally checked on him, they discovered that he wasn't exactly resting – he was dead, and his body had already begun to stiffen. He had suffered a heart attack several hours previously but no one had noticed.

THE X-FIRES

MICHAEL FAHERTY
D.O.D. 22 December 2010

Firefighters were called to an address in Galway, Ireland, after a man reported smoke pouring from a neighbour's home. When they broke in, they discovered Michael Faherty lying dead in his living room. He had burned to death, but despite his charred remains, the only visible damage to the house was to the floor beneath him and the ceiling above. The lack of evidence meant that the authorities could find no explanation for the fatal flames, and the coroner concluded it was a case of spontaneous human combustion.

SWEET SURRENDER

MITHRIDATES
D.O.D. 401 BCE

A soldier in the Persian army who killed a prince, Mithridates was sentenced to death by scaphism – or 'the boats', as it was known. He was tied up between two small boats, one on top of the other, leaving his head and limbs exposed, then force-fed milk and honey so that he would defecate or vomit, and covered in the same mixture. Then he was simply left to fester in the hot sun. Nature took its course, and after 17 days of torment he eventually died of exposure and insect infestation.

HANGING TOUGH

RAINIER HOWE
D.O.D. 4 January 1998

Twenty-year-old Rainier Howe of Melbourne, Australia, played basketball almost every night of the week, and perfected the slam dunk after years of practice. One day, he was playing with his brother and cousin when he slam-dunked the ball and hung off the ring like Michael Jordan. Unfortunately, the ring came down, along with the brick wall it was attached to, and Howe was crushed to death underneath it.

REPTILE REGRET

WAYNE ROTH
D.O.D. 8 NOVEMBER 1997

Wayne Roth was visiting a reptile collector friend who kept several large snakes in tanks when he made the serious mistake of picking up a 6-foot-long cobra, which bit him on the hand. His friend suggested he go to the hospital, but Roth told him, 'I'm a man – I can handle it.' They went to a bar instead, where he reportedly bragged about surviving the bite. He died later that evening from the slow-acting venom before his friend could drive him to the hospital.

DON'T FEED THE ANIMALS

Xu Weixing

D.O.D. 17 November 1999

Bus driver Xu Weixing was part of a convoy of vehicles carrying schoolchildren on a trip through a safari park in Shanghai when a tow rope came loose. Everyone knows that you are not even supposed to put your arm out of the window in a safari park, never mind get out of the vehicle, but apparently 41-year-old Weixing knew better, and he disembarked to reattach the rope in the tiger breeding area. Before he could finish the task, he was attacked by three Siberian tigers. By the time Weixing had been rescued, he was fatally injured, dying soon afterwards in hospital.

UP, UP AND AWAY

Reverend Adelir Antônio de Carli

D.O.D. April 2008

Father Adelir Antônio de Carli was a Catholic priest from Brazil who wanted to get closer to the heavens and raise money for charity by flying 600 miles attached to 1,000 helium party balloons. Strong winds blew him helplessly off course as he soared to an altitude of 6,000 metres, and he was last heard from when he was 30 miles offshore over the Atlantic Ocean, afraid that he would crash into the sea. Rescuers found a cluster of balloons near the priest's last known position, but his body was not located for another three months.

ALL FUN AND GAMES UNTIL SOMEONE DIES

WESLEY MITCHELL
D.O.D. 10 OCTOBER 2001

A group of students at the University of the South in Tennessee were looking for some late-night japes, so they entered the library and decided to slide down what they assumed was a laundry chute. Wesley Mitchell was the first to jump in, and he slid all the way down... into a trash compactor that switched on automatically and crushed him to death. It was not a laundry chute.

RAMMED

BETTY STOBBS
D.O.D. 28 January 1999

Farmer Betty Stobbs of County Durham was riding a quad bike to feed her sheep in a field overlooking a disused quarry. When the hungry flock got wind of the hay bale she was transporting, they surged to the vehicle and started to push it towards the edge of the quarry. Before the farmer could escape, the flock pushed her over the cliff and the quad bike fell on top of her, killing her instantly.

THE UK'S MOST DANGEROUS JOBS

Occupation	Total deaths 2010–2016	Yearly average deaths 2010–2016
Farmer	167	27.83
Builder	101	16.83
Roofer and scaffolder	69	11.5
HGV driver	41	6.83
Carpenter and decorator	28	4.66
Mechanic	26	4.33
Electrician and plumber	26	4.33
Civil engineer	20	3.33
Bin collector	20	3.33

LEAP OF FATE

Sergei Chalibashvili
D.O.D. 16 July 1983

During the diving competition at the World University Games, the sixth-placed Soviet athlete Sergei Chalibashvili attempted an ambitious reverse 3½ somersault tuck, a dive only recently approved for competition. He leapt into the air from the 10-metre tower, but as he flipped backwards, he smacked his head on the platform and fell into the water. He never regained consciousness and died of heart failure a week later.

UNDER PRESSURE

GEORGY DOBROVOLSKY, VIKTOR
PATSAYEV AND VLADISLAV VOLKOV
D.O.D. 30 JUNE 1971

Three Soviet cosmonauts were on board
the spacecraft *Soyuz 11* after time spent in
the *Salyut 1* space station. They undocked
from the station and told Control they were
preparing to return to earth. The spacecraft
completed a successful re-entry of the
earth's atmosphere and landed safely, but
when the hatch was opened, all three
cosmonauts were dead in their seats. A
valve had opened in space, causing the
cabin to rapidly depressurise. They remain
the only people to have died in space.

DOOMED FLIGHT

VLADIMIR KOMAROV
D.O.D. 24 April 1967

Soyuz 1 was a Soviet-manned space flight that was beset with problems from the start. The solo pilot was cosmonaut Vladimir Komarov, and the backup pilot was his friend, the legendary Yuri Gagarin. All unmanned test flights of the *Soyuz* craft had failed, and the two cosmonauts and engineers had serious reservations over the safety of a manned mission. However, political pressures meant that their concerns were ignored, and the mission went ahead as planned. According to reports, Komarov refused to back out despite his fears, because that meant sending his friend in his place. As soon as *Soyuz 1* was launched, issues with a solar panel meant that the ship did not have enough power to manoeuvre and could not communicate fully with earth, crippling the mission. Komarov's fate was sealed when the parachute failed on re-entry into the earth's atmosphere, leaving the craft to plummet to the ground and burst into flames, killing the cosmonaut on impact.

DEADLY ACCESSORY

ISADORA DUNCAN
D.O.D. 14 September 1927

Isadora Duncan was a flamboyant American dancer who found fame in Europe during the early twentieth century. One night, when travelling as a passenger in an open-topped car in the south of France, the long, colourful silk scarf she was wearing blew out of the cabin and became entangled in the wheels, dragging Duncan from the car and breaking her neck.

AWKWARD GUEST

Jerome I. Rodale
D.O.D. 8 June 1971

American publisher and writer Jerome I. Rodale, who advocated organic foods and healthy living, was a guest on *The Dick Cavett Show* in 1971 alongside journalist Pete Hamill. During filming, Rodale told the host that he had 'decided to live to be a hundred', and that he had never felt better in his life. When he started to snore and slump in his chair, Hamill thought Rodale was joking, but he wasn't – he was dead at the age of 72. The episode, due to be aired that night, was cancelled.

DEATH METAL

KAREN WETTERHAHN
D.O.D. 8 June 1997

Karen Wetterhahn was a chemistry professor working on the effects of toxic metals. While studying the deadly compound dimethylmercury, she accidentally spilled just one or two drops of the liquid on her rubber gloves. She removed the gloves after finishing the job, but – unknown to her – the poison had already permeated the latex and been absorbed into the skin. Wetterhahn had suffered a lethal dose, but the nature of the compound meant that the poisoning took some time to take effect, and it was several months before she realised anything was wrong and linked it to the spillage. Wetterhahn was eventually admitted to hospital with acute mercury poisoning, but treatment failed, and she died ten months after exposure.

BLADE OF GORY

VLADIMIR SMIRNOV
D.O.D. 28 JULY 1982

At the 1982 World Fencing Championships in Rome, the West German Matthias Behr was challenging the reigning champ Vladimir Smirnov of Russia. During the bout, Behr's foil snapped as he jabbed the Russian's face protector, and the jagged blade went straight through the mask, pierced Smirnov's eye socket and penetrated his brain. He was declared dead nine days later.

BLOOD SPORT

JOSÉ LUIS OCHOA
D.O.D. 30 January 2011

Cockfighting is illegal in the USA, but underground fights still take place – and it's not just the birds that are in danger. Thirty-five-year-old José Luis Ochoa suffered a fatal injury when police raided a cockfight in California in 2011. As Ochoa fled the scene, a rooster kicked him with a razor-fitted foot and sliced his leg open. Doctors were unable to stem the bleeding when he was taken to hospital, the timing of which may or may not have been delayed by the illegal nature of the activity, and he died from loss of blood.

CATA-FAULT

Dino Yankov
D.O.D. 24 November 2002

Nineteen-year-old Dino Yankov belonged to the Oxford Stunt Factory, an unofficial dangerous sports society at Oxford University. In 2002, he volunteered along with five others to be launched from a trebuchet, a giant medieval catapult. The siege weapon used a one-ton counterweight to fling people 30 metres through the air into a large net, and had reportedly done so successfully on 50 previous occasions with only one accident. The first four people hit the net safely, but bystanders were worried that they were landing too close to the edge. When Yankov was launched, their fears were realised. He clipped the edge and fell heavily to the ground, suffering multiple injuries. He died later in hospital, and the human catapult has not been used since.

DEADLY INVENTION

VALERIAN ABAKOVSKY
D.O.D. 24 July 1921

Valerian Abakovsky was the Soviet inventor of the Aerowagon, a car-like train powered by an aircraft engine coupled to a giant propeller, capable of more than 60 miles per hour. Its maiden journey from Moscow to Tula went without a hitch, but on the return leg the contraption derailed at high speed, killing seven of the 22 passengers, including Abakovsky himself. He was given the honour of being buried in the Kremlin Wall Necropolis.

TRASH CANNED

ANASTASIO FIGUEROA
D.O.D. 14 FEBRUARY 1994

Guards at a Florida prison noticed that one of their inmates was missing soon after a bin lorry had visited the facility. Lifer Anastasio Figueroa had spotted a risky opportunity to escape and jumped into the back of the truck, with predictable consequences. His crushed body was tracked down at a landfill site, and identified by his fingerprints.

BLOOD COMRADES

ALEXANDER BOGDANOV

D.O.D. 7 April 1928

Alexander Bogdanov was a Russian science-fiction writer, doctor and revolutionary, who pioneered blood transfusion during the early twentieth century. He thought sharing blood would help the workers literally bond together and extend their lives. Bogdanov gave himself several blood transfusions and claimed numerous benefits, including the prevention of baldness. When one such self-experiment used blood from a student suffering from malaria and tuberculosis, the benefits ceased.

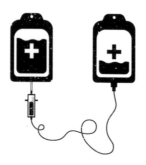

MORE UNUSUAL METHODS OF EXECUTION

- **The sack** *(ancient Rome)* – *people who had killed their parents or other close relatives were flogged and sewn into a sack with various live animals – including snakes, roosters and monkeys – then thrown into the sea.*

- **Burial** *(Europe)* – *during the Middle Ages, mothers guilty of infanticide were entombed while still alive.*

- **Hung, drawn and quartered** *(Europe)* – *in a practice used as late as the eighteenth century, criminals were dragged through the streets, hung until near death, often disembowelled, then chopped into four pieces.*

- **Death by cannon** *(India)* – *from the sixteenth century and continuing under the British empire, victims were strapped to the end of an artillery barrel and blown to pieces.*

DEADLY INGREDIENT

PENG FAN
D.O.D. AUGUST 2014

A chef at a restaurant in Guangdong, China, was preparing snake soup, the house speciality. He carefully picked the wriggling serpent out of a basket, taking care to avoid its fangs, and cut its head off. Twenty minutes later, as he threw the decapitated head away, he felt a sharp pain in his hand, and to his horror saw two puncture marks in the skin. The dead snake, a highly venomous Indochinese spitting cobra, had bitten him from beyond the grave, and he died before he could be treated. It turns out that the bite reflex of venomous snakes can be triggered hours after death, even if the head has been severed.

LAST SUPPER

BANDŌ MITSUGORŌ VIII
D.O.D. 16 January 1975

Mitsugorō was a Japanese actor, famous for his roles in kabuki theatre. He was having dinner with friends at a Kyoto restaurant when they ordered *fugu*, or pufferfish, the liver of which contains a deadly neurotoxin. Mitsugorō boasted that the poison would have no effect on him, and demanded four livers, even though the restaurant was breaking the law in serving them. He died a few hours later from the paralysing toxin, for which there is no antidote.

DID YOU KNOW?

There were 176 deaths in Japan from eating pufferfish in 1958. There are still several cases of *fugu* poisoning every year, with ten deaths recorded between 2006 and 2015.

CHECKING OUT

MILIKA SLOAN
D.O.D. 24 June 1995

A young woman from Cincinnati, Ohio, was killed by her hotel room on her first trip away from home. Milika Sloan was returning to her room, barefooted and wet from a rainstorm, when she was electrocuted as she put her key card in the door. An inspection revealed that a faulty air-conditioning unit was discharging electricity through the concrete floor and into the door frame.

ROUGH LANDING

ROGER WALLACE
D.O.D. 18 May 2002

Roger Wallace was a radio-controlled-model-plane enthusiast whose hobby would cause his death. He was flying his 5-foot-wingspan aircraft in Tucson, Arizona, when he lost sight of it in bright sunlight as it raced towards him. Wallace saw the 3-kilo plane too late to take evasive action and it struck him in the chest, causing fatal injuries.

COFFIN FIT

JOHN ORAM
D.O.D. 18 JULY 2009

When staff at a care home in Torquay heard one of their residents sneezing particularly loudly, they didn't realise it would be the end of him. But shortly afterwards, pensioner John Oram collapsed and was taken to hospital. He died two days later, and the coroner recorded that he had died from a brain aneurysm brought on by the force of a violent sneeze.

FAMOUS
LAST WORDS

....

'I've had eighteen straight whiskies;
I think that's the record.'
Dylan Thomas, poet (1953)

'They couldn't hit an elephant at this distance.'
**John Sedgwick, Union Army general, just before he was shot by a
sniper during the American Civil War (1864)**

'Codeine... bourbon...'
Tallulah Bankhead, actress and hedonist – her last request (1968)

'Pardon me, sir. I did not do it on purpose.'
**Marie Antoinette, queen of France, when she stepped on the
executioner's foot as she walked to her death at the guillotine (1793)**

'I've never felt better.'
Douglas Fairbanks, actor, after suffering a heart attack (1939)

'Go on, get out! Last words are for fools who
haven't said enough!'
**Karl Marx, revolutionary and philosopher, upon being asked by his
housekeeper for any last words (1883)**

'Tape *Seinfeld* for me.'
Harvey Korman, actor (2008)

If you're interested in finding out
more about our books, find us on Facebook
at **Summersdale Publishers** and follow us
on Twitter at **@Summersdale**.

www.summersdale.com

Image credits